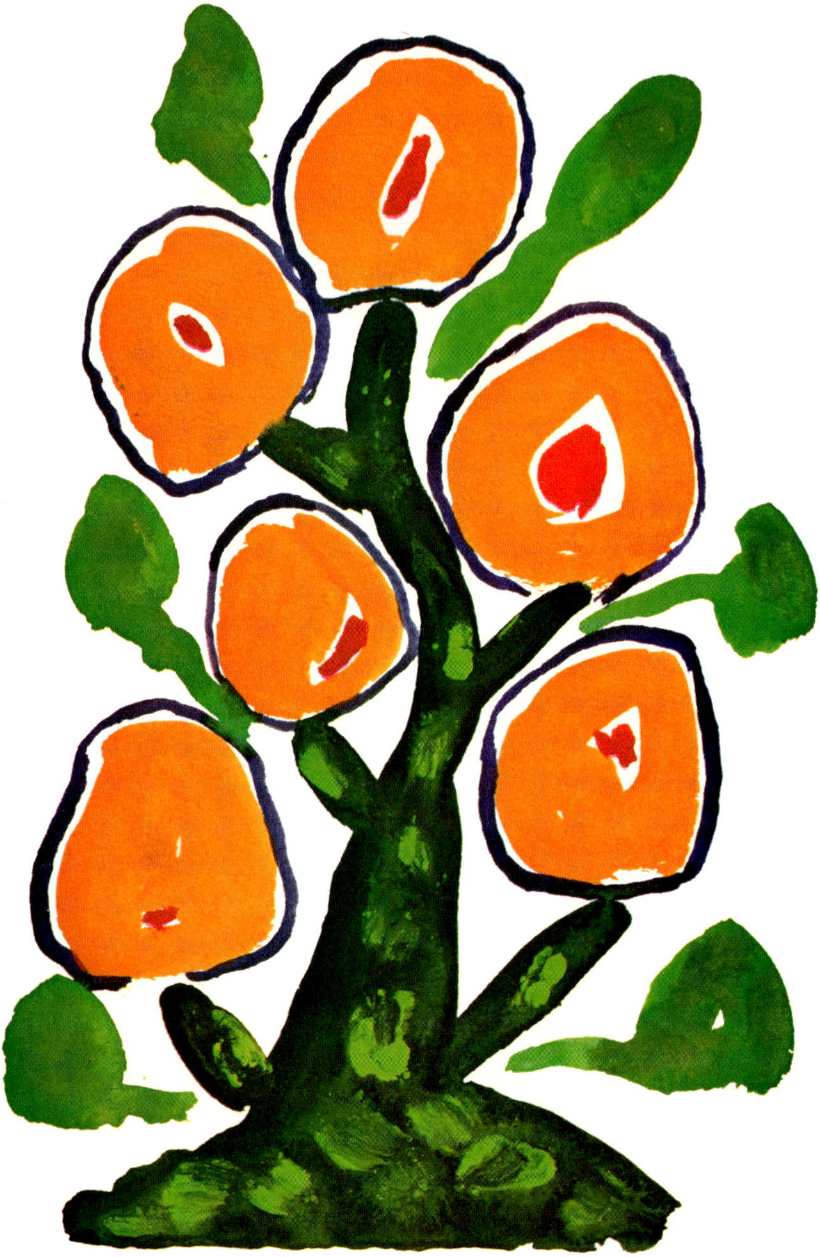

NOT ALL
I SEE IS THERE

BERNARD FORREST

los angeles
BLACK SPARROW PRESS
1970

Copyright © 1970
by Bernard Forrest

The paintings & drawings are by
the author.

SBN 87685-041-7 (paper)
SBN 87685-042-5 (signed cloth)

Not All I See Is There

A blank canvas an invitation
Her mind like that
To start with the light colors
Here and there
To end up going
out of the picture.

The river
at low tide
a strip tease
artist
soft naked
joined at the mouth
commanded
to swell and fall
by the moon

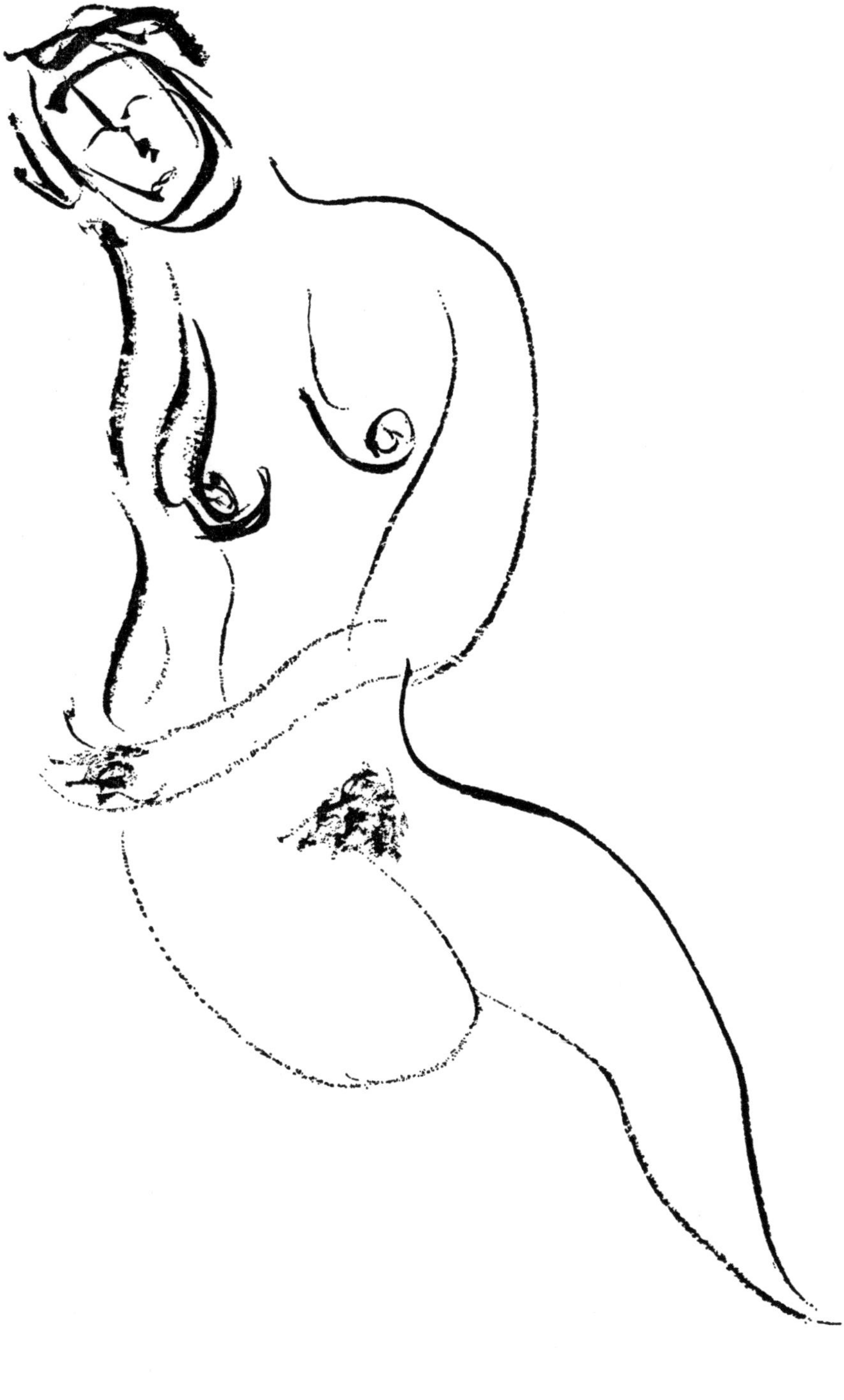

Time is
A horse
Its feet are
Strawberries
Green / on one side

SOME MEANING

My thoughts are bearded
Iris in the wind
Frail enough
To tear and come apart
Instead they move
Gayly as if they meant
Something
And were sure of themselves
Above green swords

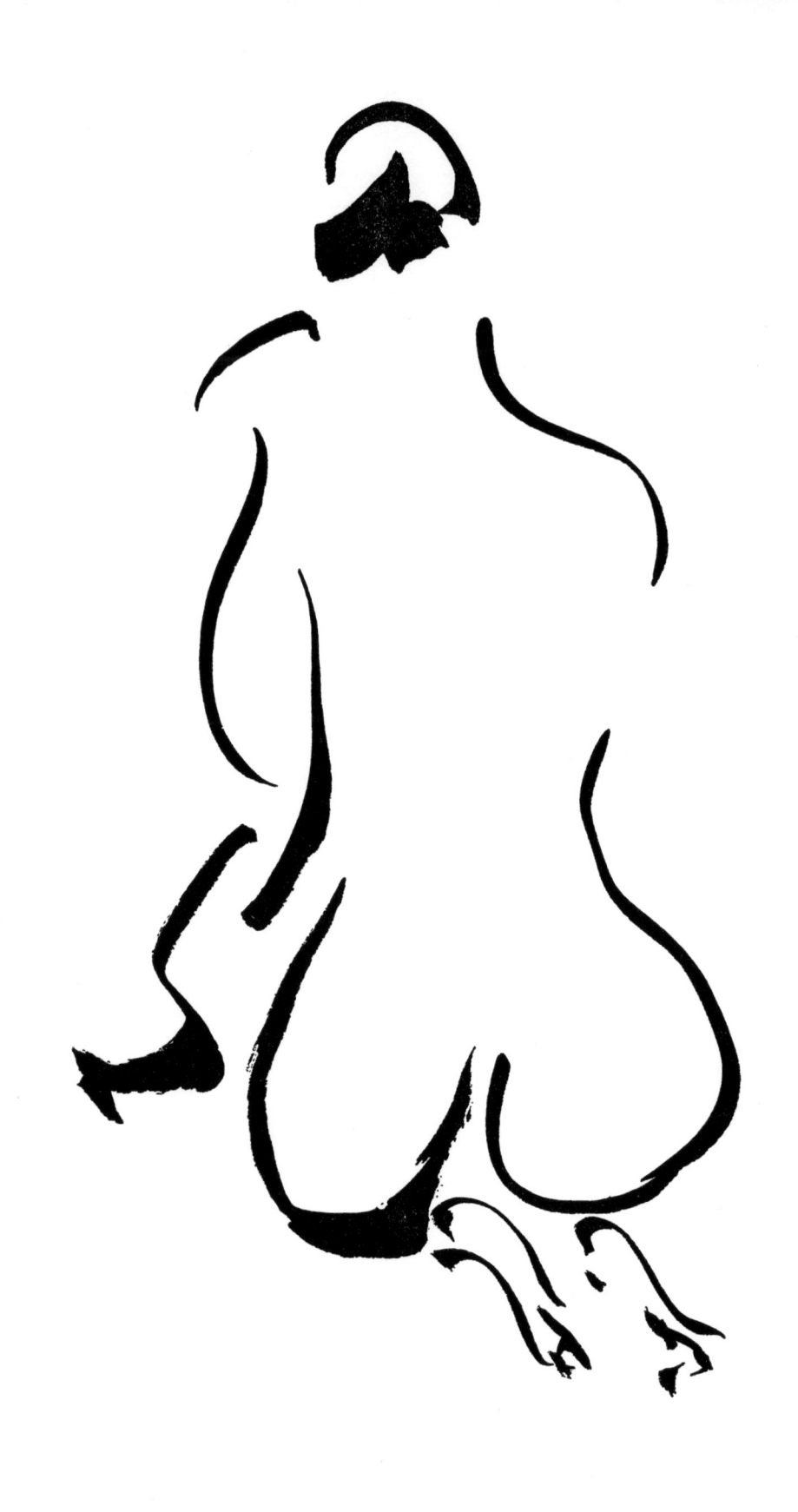

These flowers
Are dusty with
Beginnings
Again
I am with her
She has brushed
Against the flowers
And taken their stain

Here is the circumference
put in your own stars
moons suns galaxies gasses
fill in your own laser beams
atoms molecules
your own minor triumphs
a white space for a new world

look stare wonder flounder
ponder from the guide lines
the guards at the edge
warning against entrance
colored to say all
is encompassed within and without

a new world from a new world
omniscient
ready to write
on a clean
slate

the old world split spat on
pushed aside to receive and thrust
the weight of the foundation

the innocent travail
of thought coming a spring
out of a mountain

run with me into the picture
a wilderness of white
free the hot line
the lightning
flashes
a new world
wanting form

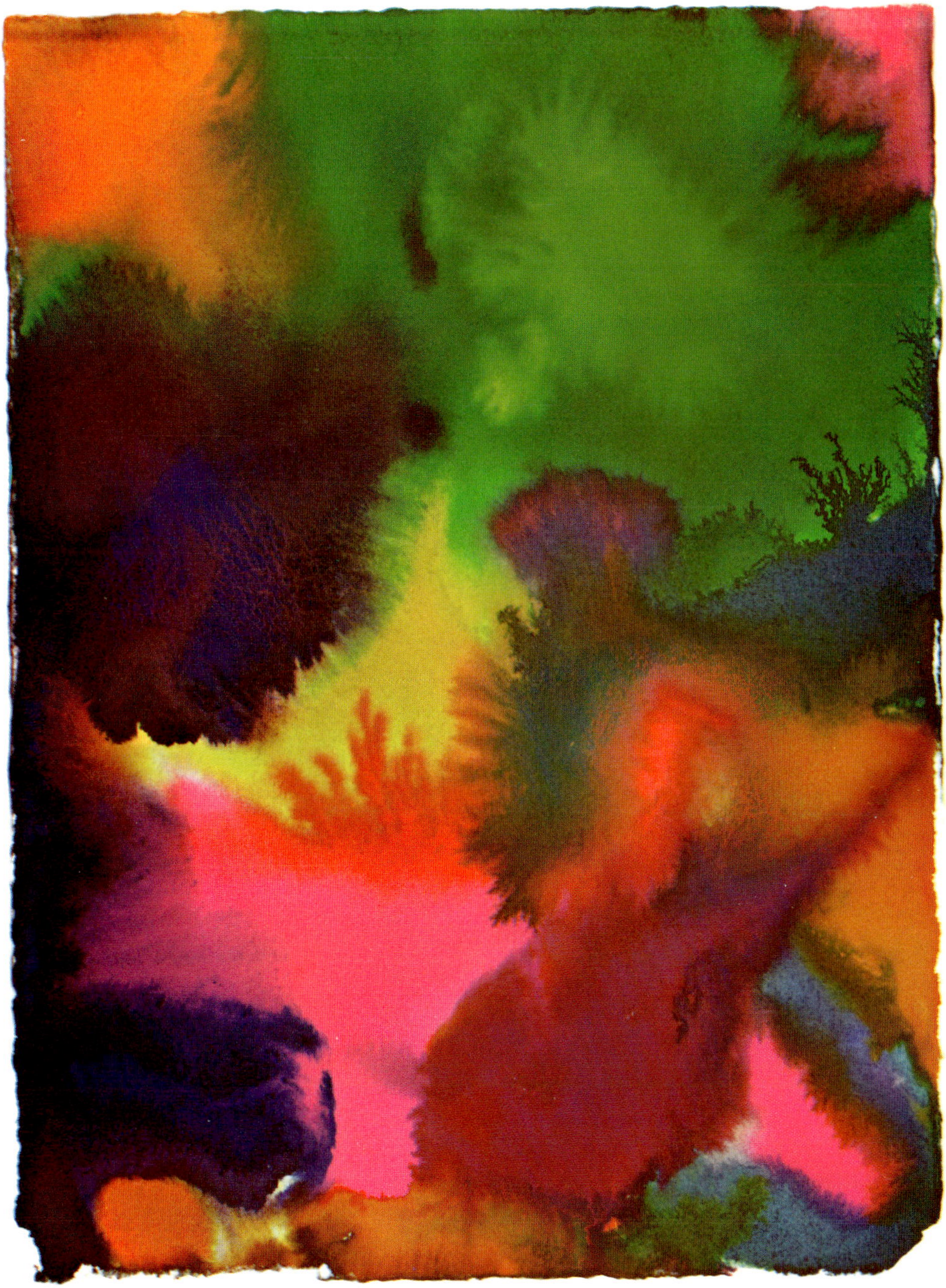

Not ripe
The fruit hangs
Look for my word
It is not enough
Someone else
Is in it the net
Is on it
The escape from it
Ultimate doorway
Opens to winter
Do not scratch
The window panes
Frosted to compete
With the freeze
Swear you saw it
You the witness
The less ready
Nonsense
On the table
Seagulls at
Floor forty two

O NO

She was like cardboard
That could be cut into sizes
And shaped if dampened a little
And I wanted to tell her this
But my friend said
She would not understand
And I said
Can I say she is like a rose
And he said O God no

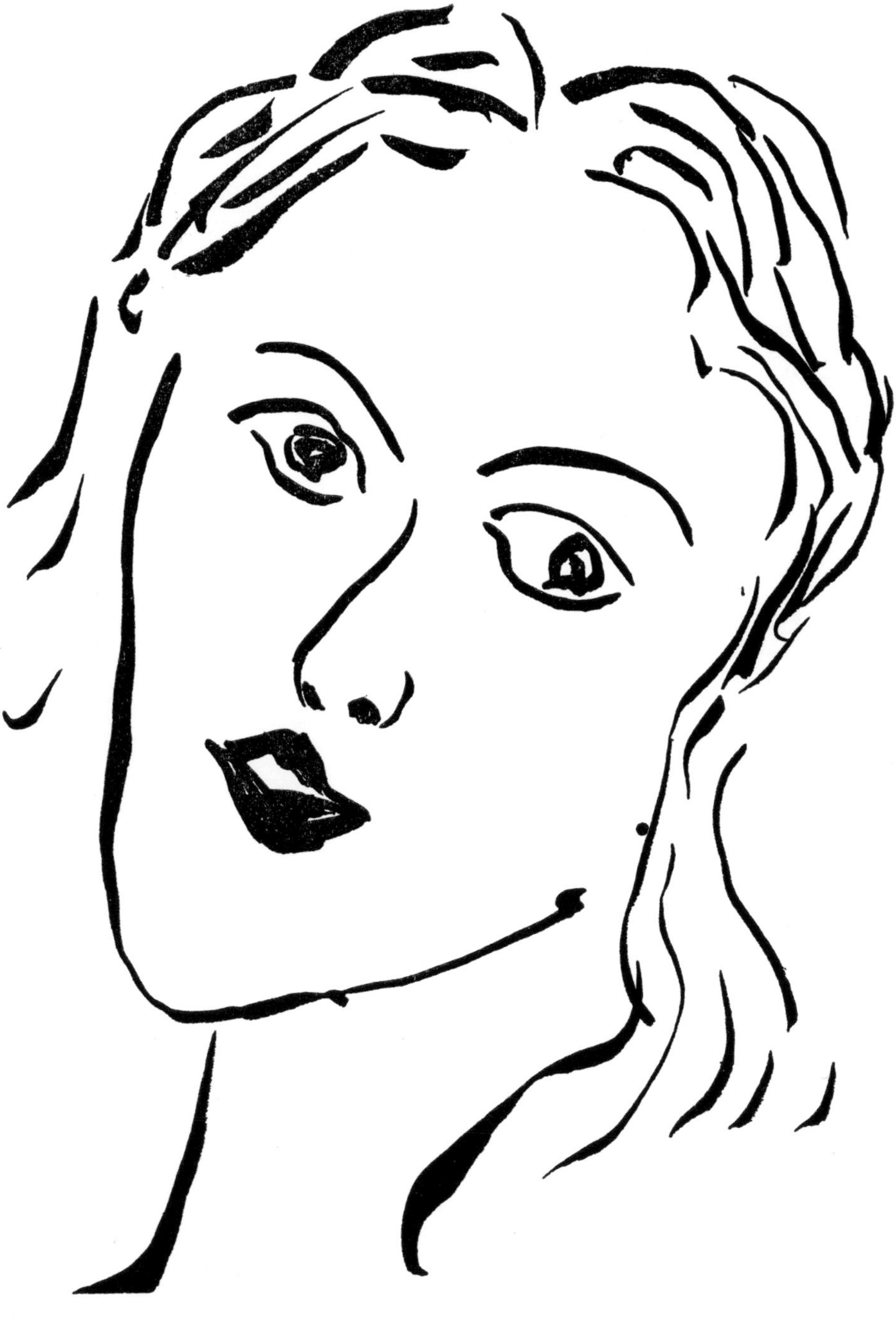

GEESE GOING

Geese going
South
White alders in leaf
The same
Each year
But far enough
Between
Each
To wait for each
To come
And go
The white
Geese
Know this
Flying
In formation
Honking their
Way to glory

GUADALAJARA

Two sacks of sugar each
Eight hundred sacks
Four hundred mules
That's the mathematics
    They all stop
    In the same
    Stinking place
With sugar
On the way to Guadalajara

She smiled and I said hello
And asked her
What she represented
A person should
And she said you tell me first
I said come with me
And she said
No thank you
The polite bitch

Sam
you say that words are out of date
and color is in as it slips away
for you to the outside
and you make a void
for music
and speak out
in a way that is less foreign
for knowing you

but you picked out brushes
and paper for me
and said try it yourself
fair enough
and some day perhaps
I will have been taught
to talk back
without words

what am I to do meanwhile
to shed the past
coil up in a corner
ready to strike out
without knowing why

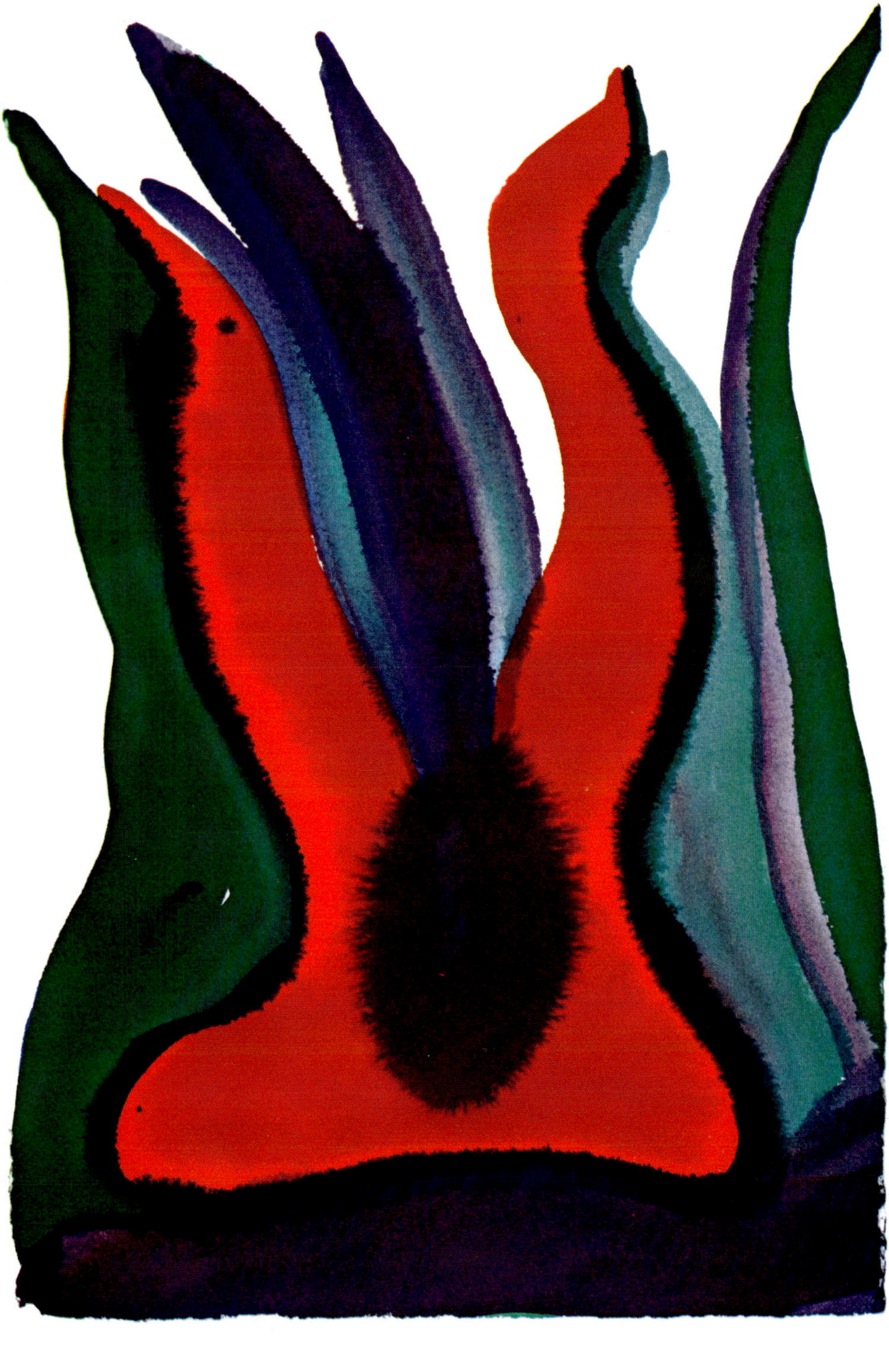

I sit congested
like an owl
or a snake

1

Comes to me as a shock
A banana an apple
This blond woman with loose teeth
The passage of time my old days slip away
My feet wear out
I need thicker glasses
More inquisitive
As the chances increase
Men in a tank on the sea bottom
Porpoises moving under water

2

A light show coming
Out of the ground in torrents
A water fall going backwards and forwards
Cows down to the water
Snakes in a pit bowed
Round each other and the trunk
Of a tree growing upside down
Time fluctuating between day and night
No longer passing catching
Up with itself
Comes to me as a shock
A canteloupe or a grapefruit

Soft voices
follow the wind
leave space
for me as if I
was in need

SILENCE

This is my silence
My lake
That has not lapped
Against the sand
Of the edge
Where there are no reeds
To hide a bird from the talk
Or the binoculars

This is my silence
Against these boulders
That stand or lie
Along a foothill of granite
Long since given
Over to jackrabbits
And quail

My silence broken
By a scuffle of feet
Following a nose down
Like a gopher
Going away from the sun

My silence which is
My way of words
Like the silence of vapor
Trails blown across
The sky before night falls

Her gentleness
in change
before dark
take words
without teeth

EMPTINESS

The clothes hanging
Behind white sliding doors
Or on bodies
At wax works
Or on effigies in museums
Or on kings and queens buried
With fame and honour
Below hot sands
Are voices of emptiness

What is Sam Francis
doing to the world
he has seen and smelt
something perfect like
a dog
and held it

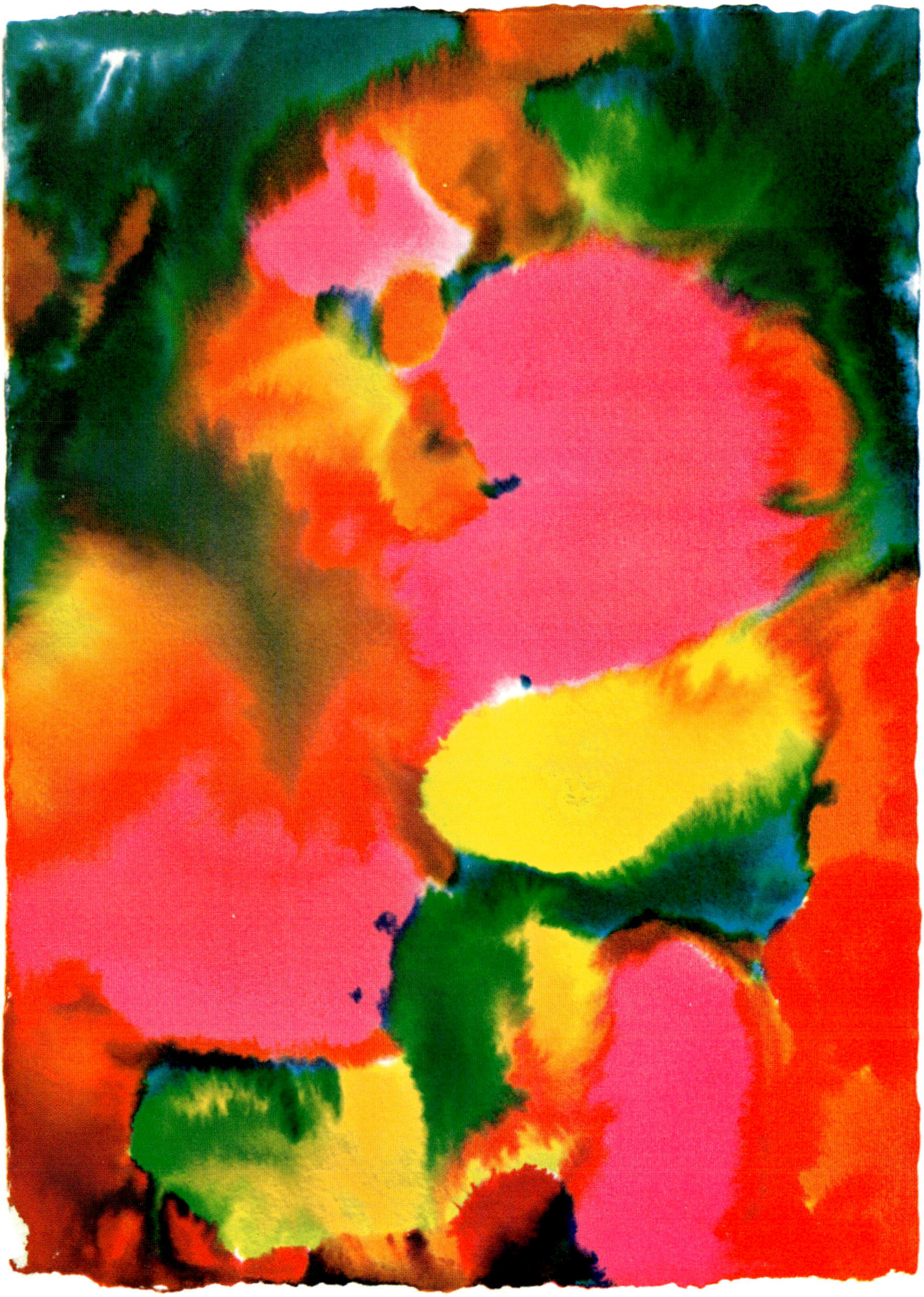

I ask a stranger to model for me
And she says she will
And next time I see her
She stares at me
And we say hello

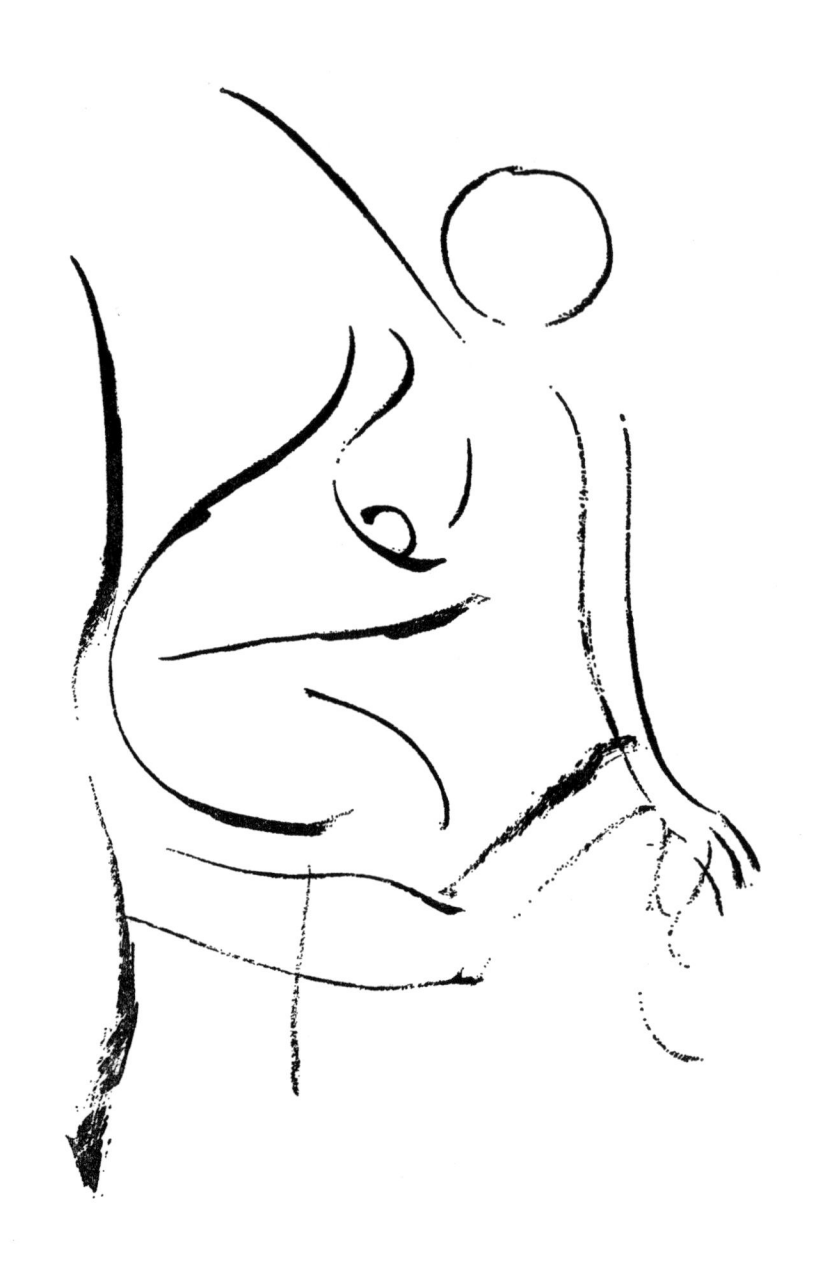

This girl is
As my friend says
Not
Beautiful but I say
That what is not
One thing can be another.

A girl with her mind
Laid over her arm
Like a dress back
From the laundry
Her mouth moist in circles
Clockwise and counter
Clockwise
And when she speaks it sounds
As if her thoughts were thrown
Over her arm.

There is an albatross
flying at my left elbow
one eye is shut
the other is
forming the horizon

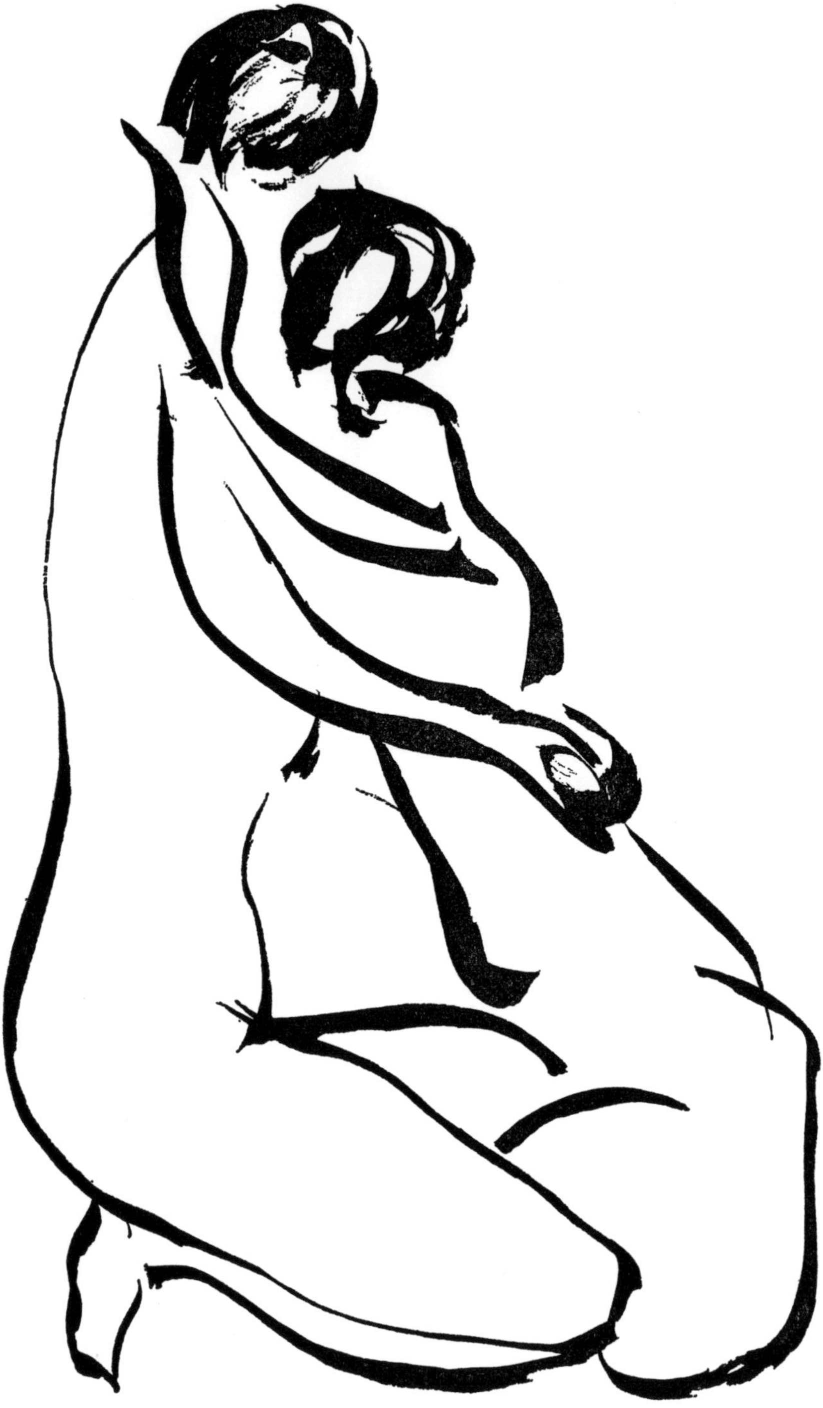

Our hands explore
Make promises
Find ways without words
To tempest
(Sounds of) victory
And silence

WHATEVER

There is in front of me
Whatever it is
Such as windows painted
And colored against
Whatever
And I am not looking
In front of me for anything
Nor am I asking for anything
Nor am I listening for any form of truth
And whatever you say floats
Past me in the sky like
A balloon sent up to find
Out about the weather
To brush against the sun
And I am full of something
That I cannot understand
But whatever it is
Is against me and sorrow
And I am thinking
How fortunate I am
To be full of something
Whatever it is
Against trouble and tears

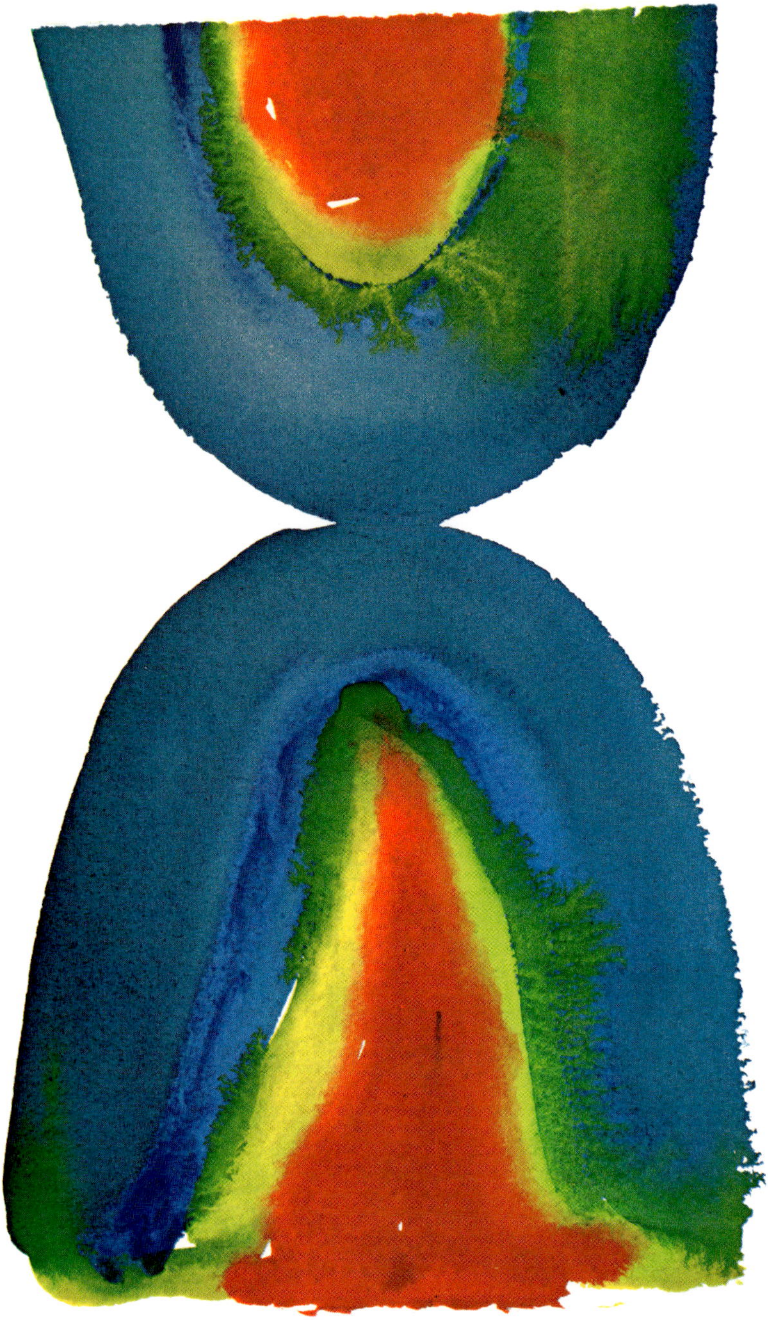

MIDNIGHT

Warmth
My dog
No
I am in luck
With a stranger

BECAUSE OF HER

There is something to say
Because of her
But it has not been said
Because of her
The waters have taken in the lights
They have taken in the stars
And moonlight
But they have not taken in everything
Because of her
She is standing before a fire
Before her eyes
Their colour hidden
There is silence
Because of her

The Oriental girl
Has gone away
To say nothing
In another world.

Or, if her voice
Is not lost
She is faced
Toward the new moon
And has forgotten
That it shines behind
As well as in front of her.

And as I look at it
The words I have for her
Fail to leave me
And I stand in silence.

The sea takes more than it
Gives back
And takes back what is taken
From it.
It can be stretched into a white
Wake that rocks
Idly and disintegrates
Its fury; and its moods
Are borrowed, and it fades back
As it is told.
As so many do not.

I tell my dog about easter
He listens carefully
He goes out
To piss on a white rose.

WAITING IN SILENCE

Beneath pear trees
I have stood saying
Lord lord and no
Wind has whispered
I have waited by willows
For voices in silence
I have called out but there
Has been no echo
From the hills
The clocks
Have run on
What has been forbidden
Continues without forgiveness
And what has been forgiven
Is no longer wanted
The hills are damp
In sadness

An old man shakes

The fruit turns

as illiterate
on one side as the other

She took my leaves graciously
She smelled them and asked
What they were and she put
Them down on the table and that
Is where they are now
Or would be if I had not thrown
Them away

She took my leaves graciously
She smelled them saying oh I know
How lovely and she put them
In her purse and I am still
Looking for her

She took my leaves and kept them
In her hand for a time and dropped
Them discreetly at the garden door

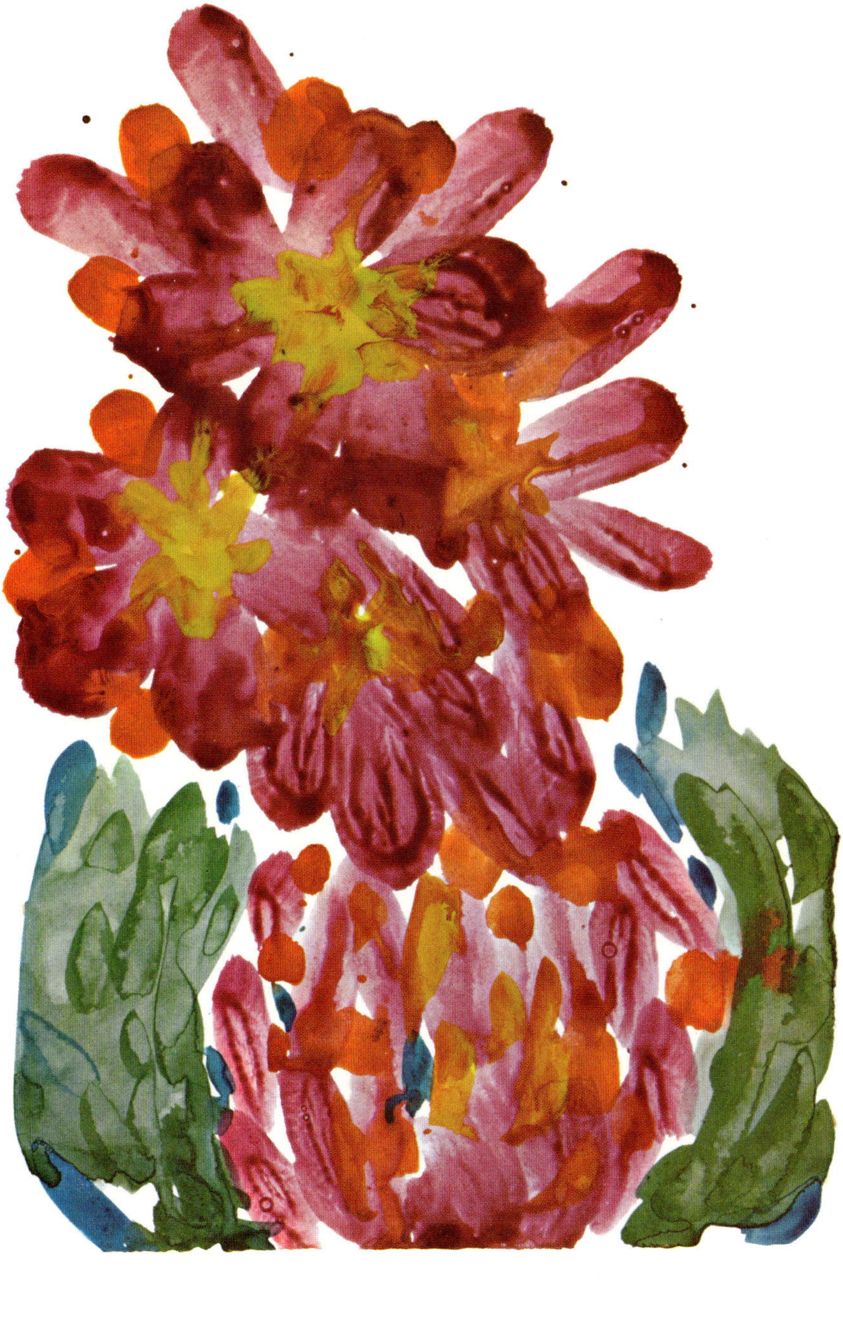

Matilija soft
White poppy paper to touch
Early summer sun

I stumbled over a stone
which was smooth and communicative
it turned into someone I wanted to see
and I found that I was on two roads
at the same time

a warning

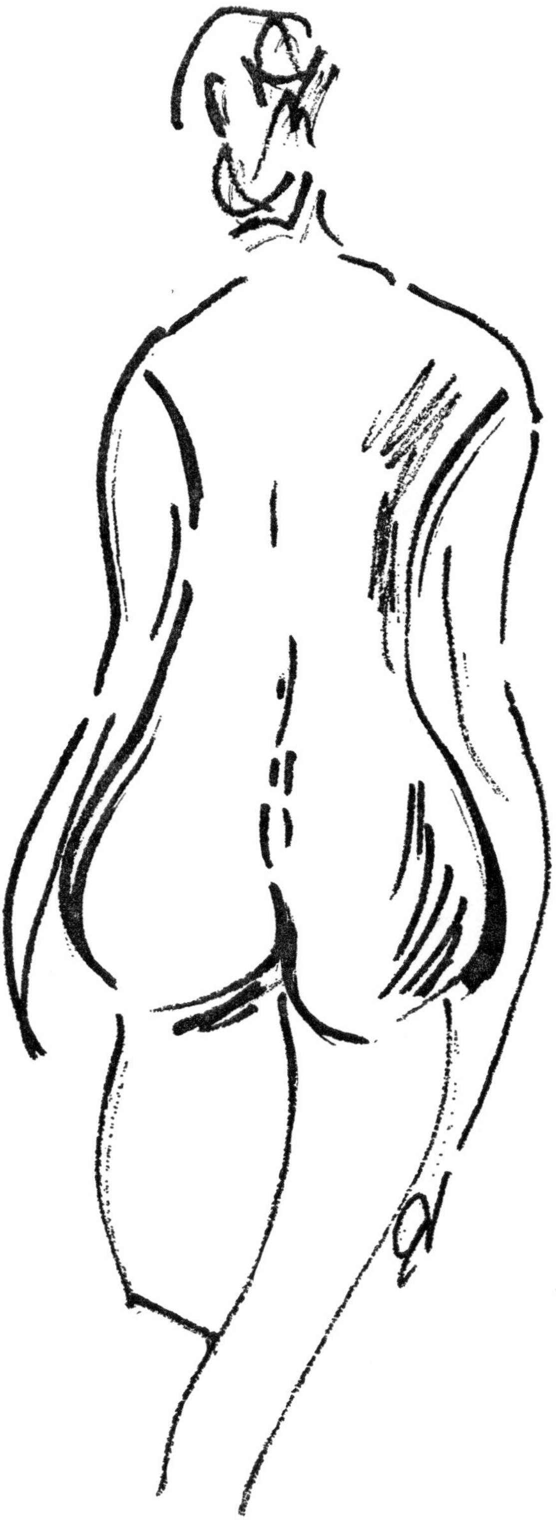

SCULPTOR

As you would
I would like
    To find words
        Like wind speaking
        Through knot holes
Or hail stones
Big as eggs
Landing on tin barns
    And nurse them
    Back to life
    In a deep freeze
So they come
Out silent
And could be
Chiselled into meaning

CARAVAN

Gypsy colors
Cloth buttons cut
Music minds
A house on wheels
On no mans land
Not far from my
Chickens not far
From my children
The music good
Or evil and they
Want pots and pans
And my knives for
Sharpening or something

The sun shines on her
It could not do otherwise
The glistening snow

Haiku (handwritten)

WITHOUT

I have traveled without signs
And without a companion
The days and nights have
Not been fulfilled
I have stood before the water
Falls in silence

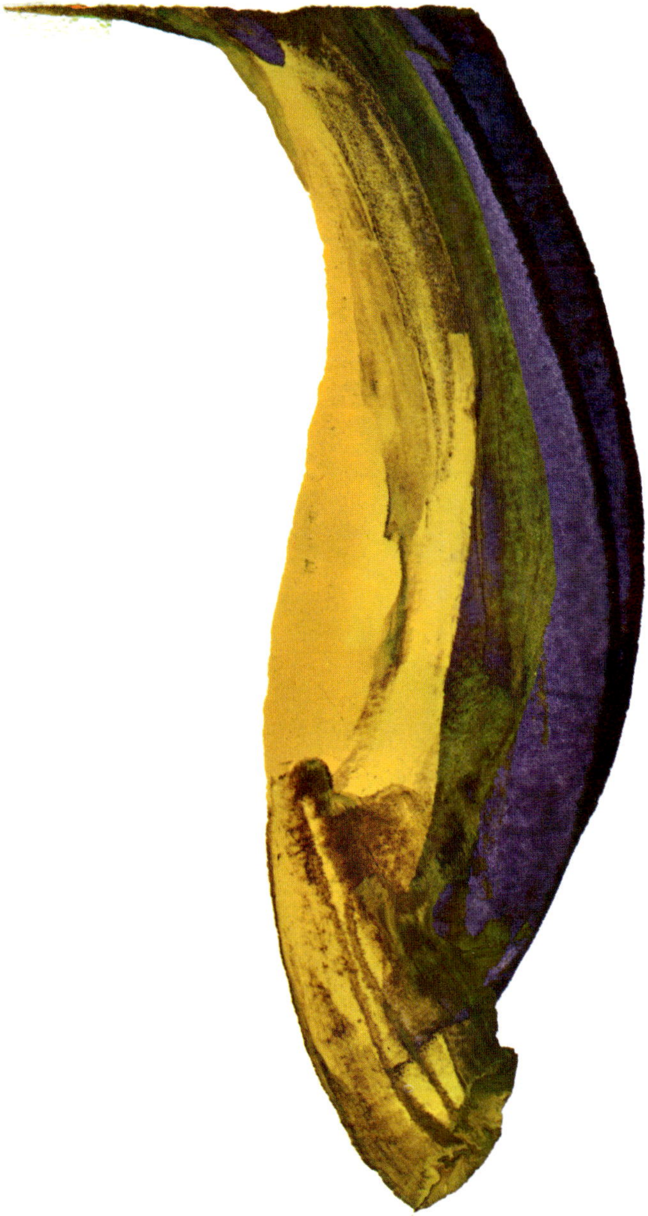

GUARDIAN

Beauty is here
The green mown lawn
Running down
To meadows falling
In the sea
The house a placid
Guardian of the scene
Stands pleasantly
Between the trees
And there is quiet
Except for gently rolling seas
And in the firs a breeze
But this is not all
There is a spirit moves
Within the house
Which proves more
Than the eyes and ears approve
For all inside is magical
And will allow
Nothing to dwell within
But love now

He had silent songs
Which he sang against silence
Crows in the morning

Snow deeper than thought
Had fallen everywhere
Hiding newspapers

NIGHT BLOOMING CEREUS
(epiphyllum oxypetalum)

In my garden
At midnight
In absolute silence
White flowers
Come unattended
They offer their
Sweetness to the moon
And wait for moths
Daughters of chance
Ready to bow
Before the sun

Look at legs
The words come through shoes
Gathering meaning
From bones and marrow

Moving toward hot water
To remove sweat and whiskers
And try for a match
Of word against word
Or look against look
Or perhaps silence
And only the sense
Of water flowing round
My feet so that
Some time and not soon
I hope
I shall walk
On warm water
To judge
To convict
And say go to go to

A girl sits on stones
The moon shines in her green eyes
I remain asleep

She is as I see her
Lost in her special way
Not in wilderness
But in a garden that has
No flowers

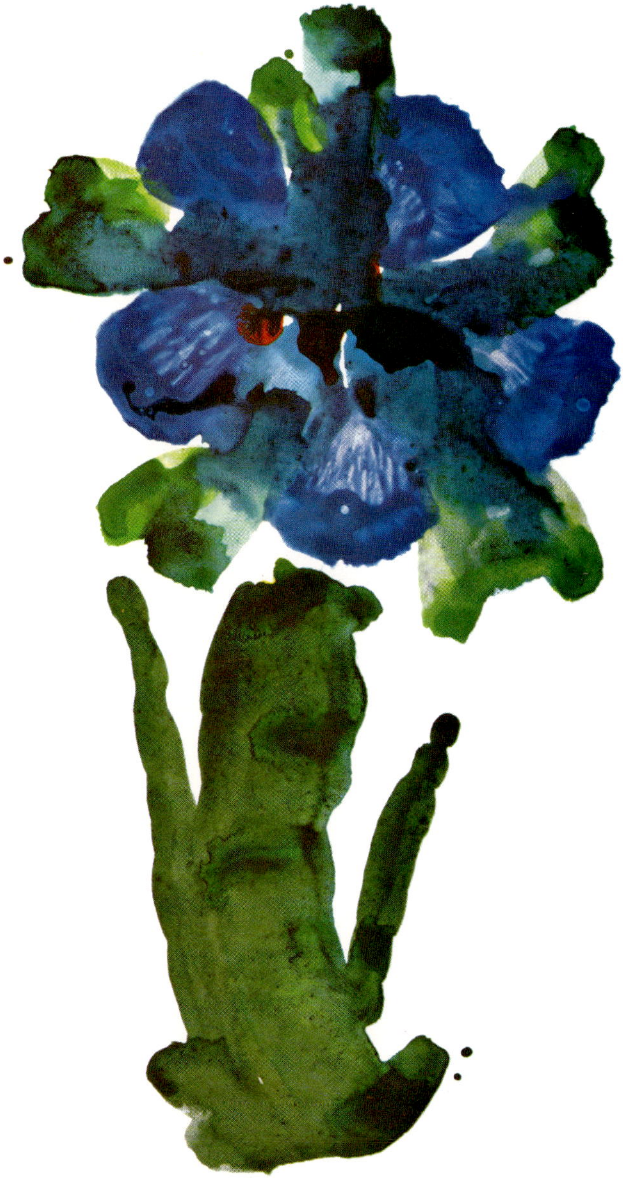

She said nothing to me
I started to say nothing
Birds against sunset

BEYOND

The stage
An empty
Space beyond
Stars having
To go round
Again and the moon
Dragging its heels
Suffering cold starved

Ships at the dock
Bananas entirely
Green chrysalises
Hiding beauty
And voices to say
They alone know
The winches and donkey
Engine the need
To be off loaded

The french cabin
Louis Quatorze
In the tropics
The captain
And the hidden woman
Who cares

Voices
Beneath boards
Long steps
Toward an unwanted
Future but ready
With hands and feet
If not rotted

Music always distant
Again in the background
The voice not raised
But unmistakable

There are rings
For my ankles
The height of bilge
Waters rising
Taken at levels
By whining pumps

Persistent smells
Rising and falling
As if
By command
Under feet
Dancing
I can only think
Of how it is
Without me

It is over
As if the sun
Shone after a thunderstorm
I cannot tell
How long ago
The dark skies
Tree silhouette
Green on green
One and another
Always beyond

We could feed
Cattle and sheep
Collect eggs and feathers
And watch seeds in the wind

Not
All
I see
Is
There

Printed June 1970 in Santa Barbara by Noel Young for the Black Sparrow Press. Design by Barbara Martin. This edition is limited to 750 copies bound in paper wrappers & 200 large paper copies handbound in boards by Earle Gray signed & with an original watercolor by the author.

Poet and painter Bernard Forrest is the author of three previous books, including *Not meaning not to see*, the first book published by the Black Sparrow Press. His poems have appeared in a number of magazines and have been anthologized.

Photo: KIRA GODBE